G000161534

Life as a...

Medieval Peasant

F.J Beerling

Illustrated by Gareth Bowler

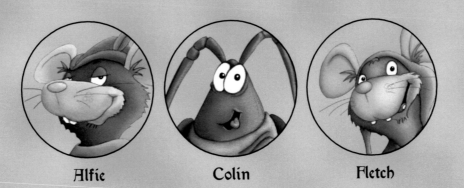

Alfie   Colin   Fletch

© Copyright F.J. Beerling/Gareth Bowler 2015
Fairyfaye Publications
ISBN: 9780993384219

Happy Reading!
2016

First paperback edition

ISBN: 9780993384219

Published by Fairyfaye Publications
For events and all enquiries email fairyfayepublications@gmail.com

Edited by Denise Smith www.dspublishingservices.co.uk

With thanks
to Professor Louise Wilkinson, Professor of Medieval History at The Canterbury Christ Church University for the verification of the historical content in this book.

www.fairyfayepublications.co.uk

Designed & set by Gareth Bowler

Printed in Great Britain

Once upon a long ago, when ancient Rome had crumbled,
Across the Medieval streets the carts and horses rumbled.

Dodging lots of pee and plop, you were covered in poo galore;
The upstairs toilet had been invented, a hole cut through the floor.

Clothing was hung in the toilet, though not if you were a peasant,
To stop the moths from chewing them;
even they found poo unpleasant!

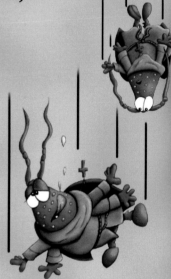

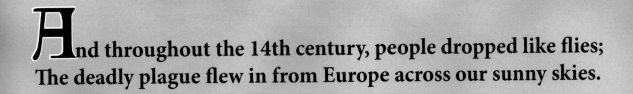

$\mathcal{A}$nd throughout the 14th century, people dropped like flies;
The deadly plague flew in from Europe across our sunny skies.

Yes, these were the Middle Ages, when peasants were pongy and poor,
Paying their taxes to bad King John who taxed them even more!

You shared your home with dirty animals and bedded in their hay
To stop the poachers stealing them and stop them wandering away.

The house was smelly and made of poo, mixed with soil and straw,
Then plastered onto a wooden frame, with a curtain for the door.

The roof was covered in layers of straw;
repairs were quick and easy,
With windows cut into the plaster
to stop you feeling queasy.

Laundry day was just as smelly but bleaching worked a treat,
Clothes were soaked in buckets of pee then trampled by your feet.

By now your hands were covered in germs; time to cook the tea,
But not before you wiped your bottom and poisoned the family!

Yes, this is how diseases spread throughout the Middle Ages,
Cholera, dysentery, measles and plague, the list could fill up pages!

But not all peasants dropped down dead, some would
farm the earth,
Renting land from the Lord of a Manor; the farmer was called a Serf.

Now, the serf was just a pongy peasant who wore a pointy hat
And, according to some historians, was probably taxed for that!

Tax for the grain they harvested and ovens to bake their bread,
Even a tax to cross the bridge and a tax if you wanted to wed!

The Peasants had to pay the church and farm their land for free
They had to obey their local lord as they had few rights to plea.

In fact they had very little and never cleaned their teeth,
As if that wasn't bad enough, I bet they were all called "Keith"!

Being a peasant and called Keith,
   you probably paid more tax,
Although you find this hard
      to believe,
      these are medieval facts!

The peasants grew tired of being smelly and living a life of poo,
Paying taxes and being called Keith, so decided on what to do.

They filled a document with good ideas and gave it to the king.
"Sign it or die," declared his barons, "you cannot rule everything."

No longer were peasants sent to jail without a very good reason,
Like being naughty, stealing the cattle or committing treason.

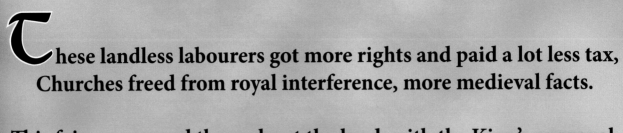

These landless labourers got more rights and paid a lot less tax,
Churches freed from royal interference, more medieval facts.

This fairness spread throughout the land, with the King's approval,
But bad King John, he never played fair,
thus leading to his removal.

All thanks to this one document,
originally called "The Big Charter",
But everything sounds better
in Latin, so here's to......

The Magna Carta!!!

Can you help the cockroaches answer these questions in this Medieval Peasant quiz?

1. Where was clothing hung?

A: On a washing line   B: In the toilet   C: In a wardrobe

2. What flew in from Europe?

A: An aeroplane   B: Two rats in a balloon   C: The deadly plague

3. What did you share your home with?

A: The neighbours   B: Smelly animals   C: Bananas

4. What did you soak your clothes in?

A: The bath   B: Chocolate milkshake   C: Buckets of wee

5. How were diseases spread throughout the Middle Ages?

A: By cockroaches   B: By post   C: By not washing your hands

6. What was a medieval farmer called?

A: A serf   B: A surfer   C: A dung beetle

7. Who did peasants have to pay money too?

A: Their mobile phone bill   B: The church   C: A piggy bank

8. What did the peasants grow tired of?

A: Watching paint dry   B: Waiting for a bus   C: Being smelly

9) What did the peasants give to the king?

A: A document of good ideas   B: A very bad cold   C: Sausages

10. What was the Magna Carta originally called?

A: The Big Charter   B: The Big Piece of Paper   C: The Alfie and Fletch Annual 1379

Answers. 1:B   2:C   3:B   4:C   5:C   6:A   7:B   8:C   9:A   10:A

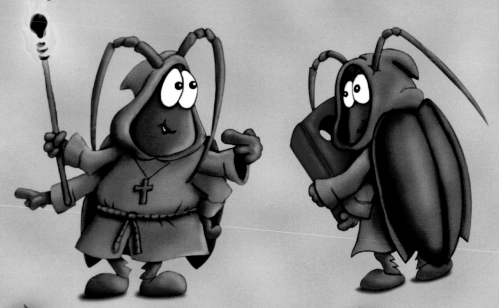

Faye Beerling grew up in a children's home, which was full of children and not a lot of toys. To amuse herself Faye developed a big imagination and has made a living out of it ever since. Faye also loves history and decided to combine the two. The result is books for children that are engaging, educating and entertaining.

Gareth Bowler didn't grow up and drew this book. He went to Art College in the 15oo's and failed. After several uneventful years drawing bears, Gareth now specialises in rat and cockroach illustration.